21st Century
Basic Skills
Library

I KNOW HOCKEY

by Joanne Mattern

Cherry Lake Publishing • Ann Arbor, Michigan

3

Published in the United States of America
by Cherry Lake Publishing
Ann Arbor, Michigan
www.cherrylakepublishing.com

Consultant: Marla Conn, Read-Ability

Library of Congress Cataloging-in-Publication Data
Mattern, Joanne, 1963-
  I know hockey / Joanne Mattern.
     pages cm. -- (I know sports)
   ISBN 978-1-62431-401-8 (hardcover) -- ISBN 978-1-62431-477-3 (pbk.) --
ISBN 978-1-62431-439-1 (pdf) -- ISBN 978-1-62431-515-2 (ebook)
1. Hockey--Juvenile literature. I. Title.
   GV847.25.M334 2013
   796.962--dc23
                                        2013006125

Cherry Lake Publishing would like to acknowledge
the work of The Partnership for 21st Century Skills.
Please visit *www.p21.org* for more information.

Printed in the United States of America
Corporate Graphics Inc.
July 2013
CLFA11

TABLE OF CONTENTS

History

Hockey is a great sport to play in the cold. It can be played outside or inside.

Hockey started more than 200 years ago. People used sticks to hit a ball. Now players play with a **puck**.

The first indoor hockey game was played in 1875. Today, most hockey games are played on indoor **rinks**.

Playing the Game

Players skate up and down the ice. They use their sticks to pass and shoot the puck.

Both teams try to shoot the puck into the other team's goal. The goal is six feet (1.8 m) wide in professional hockey. **Goalies** try to keep the puck out.

The game moves very fast. Teams battle to control the puck. They switch from **offense** to **defense** quickly.

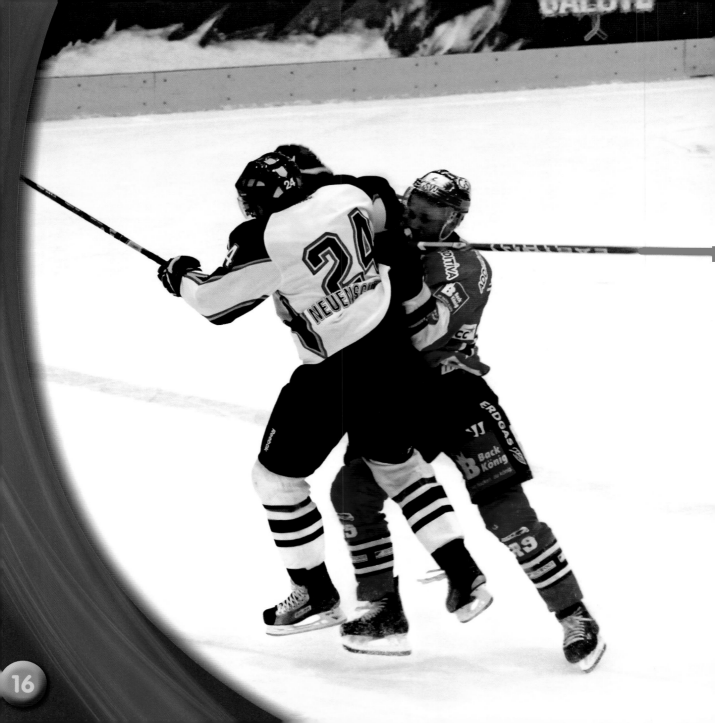

Safety

Hockey is a rough sport. Players wear special gear to stay safe. They wear thick gloves and body pads.

All players wear helmets.
Young players also wear
face masks.

A goalie wears bigger, thicker pads. These pads help block shots and keep the goalie safe.

Find Out More

BOOK

Roza, Greg. *Hockey*. New York: Gareth Stevens, 2012.

WEB SITE

Sports Illustrated Kids

www.sikids.com

This Web site has articles about professional hockey teams and players.

Glossary

defense (DEE-fens) players who try to stop the other team from scoring

goalies (GOH-lees) the players who stay in the goal to stop the other teams from scoring

offense (AW-fens) players who try to score

puck (PUK) a small disk made of rubber

rinks (RINGKS) enclosed areas with smooth surfaces where people can skate and play hockey

Home and School Connection

Use this list of words from the book to help your child become a better reader. Word games and writing activities can help beginning readers reinforce literacy skills.

ago	goal	outside	started
ball	great	pass	sticks
block	hit	play	switch
cold	hockey	puck	teams
control	ice	rough	thick
down	inside	safe	today
fast	keep	shoot	up
first	most	skate	wear
games	moves	special	years
gear	now	sport	

Index

About the Author

Joanne Mattern loves all sports. She likes hockey games because the action is so fast. Joanne has written biographies of many athletes. She lives with her family in New York State.